Happy Faces

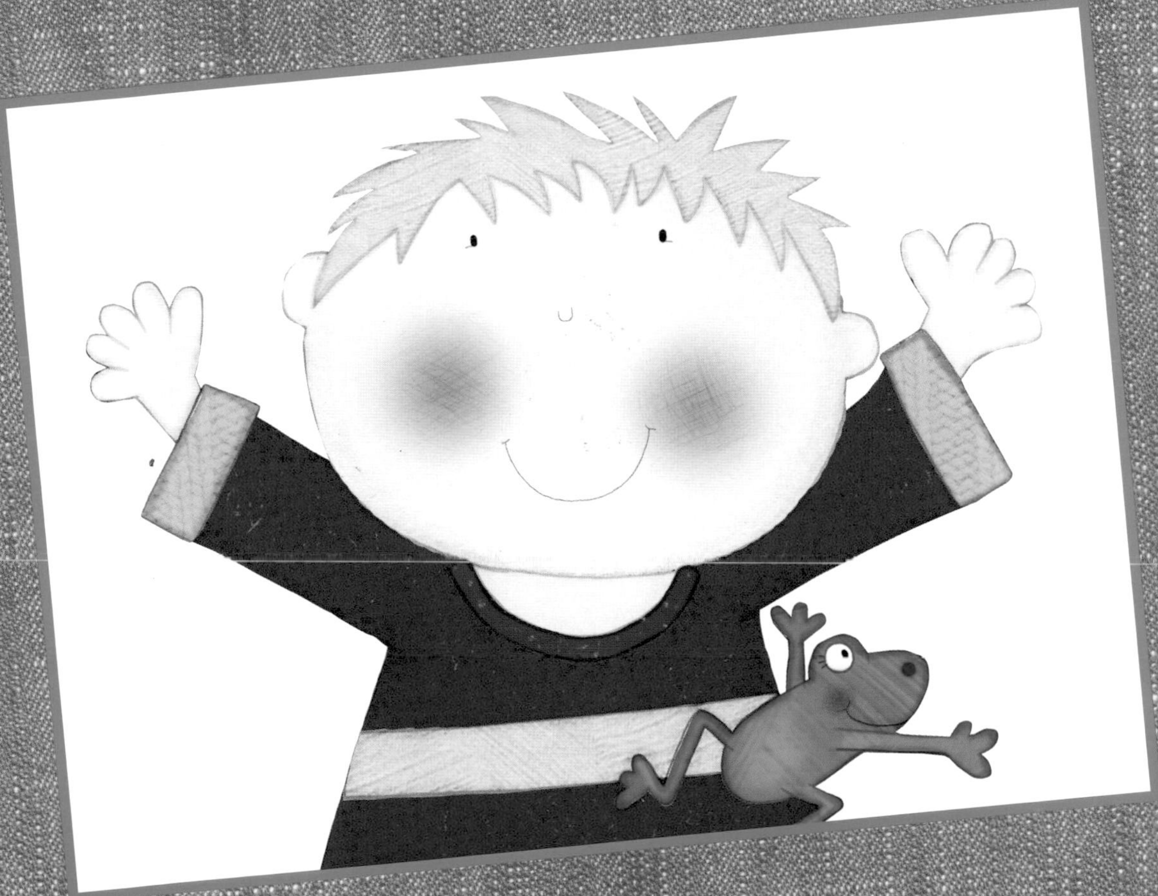

Parragon

Bath New York Singapore Hong Kong Cologne Delhi Melbourne

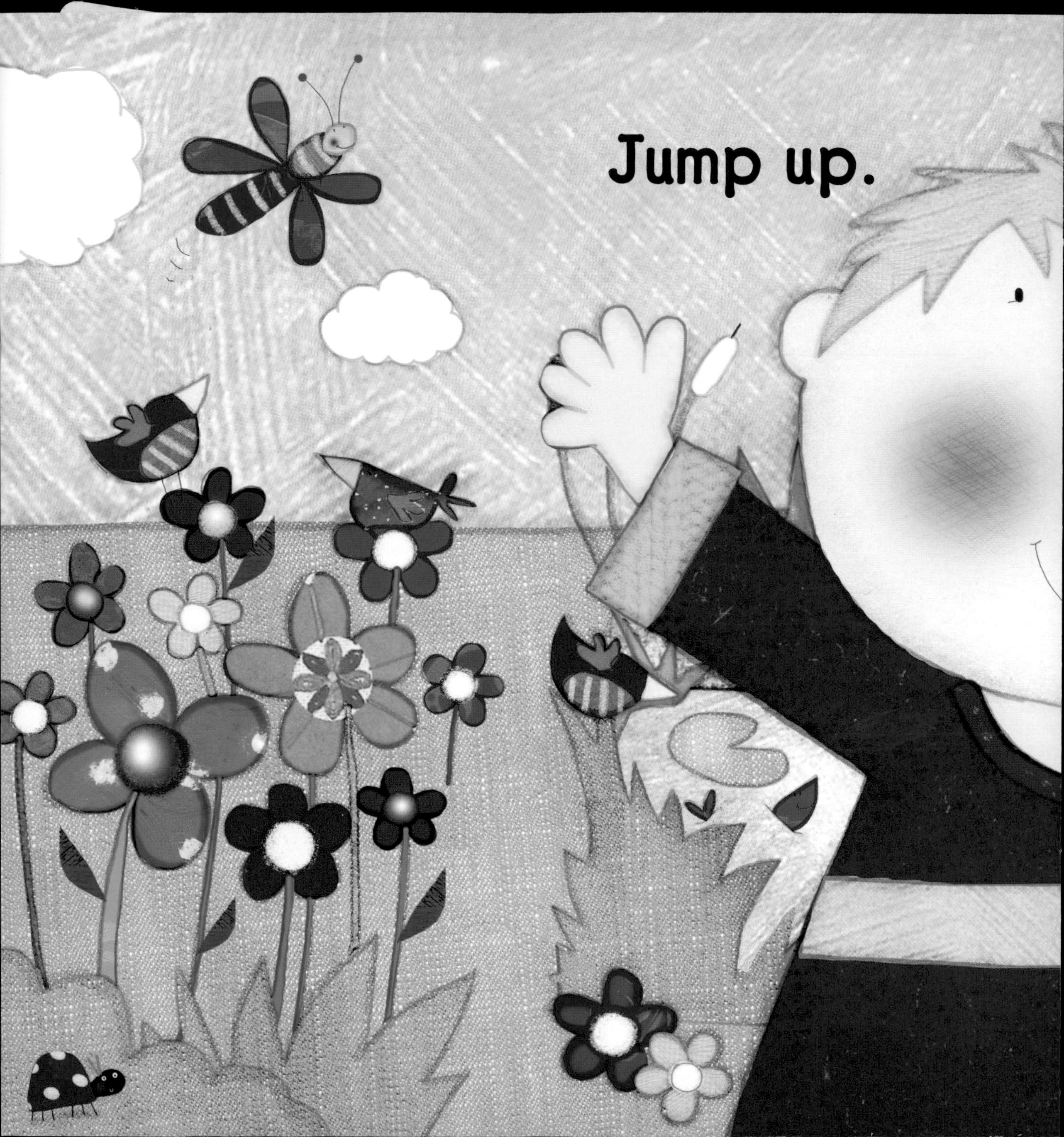

Jump up.

Hello!

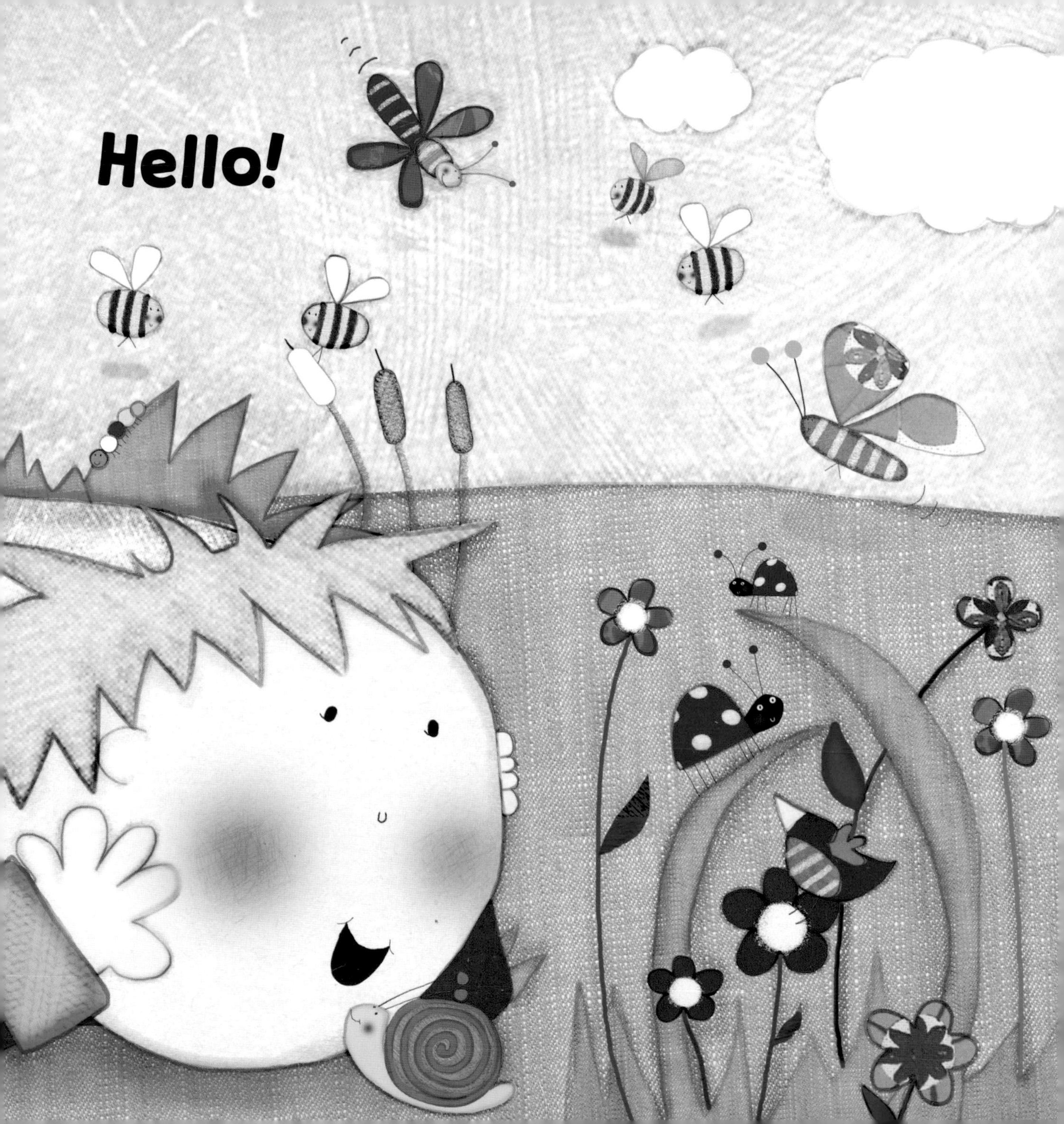

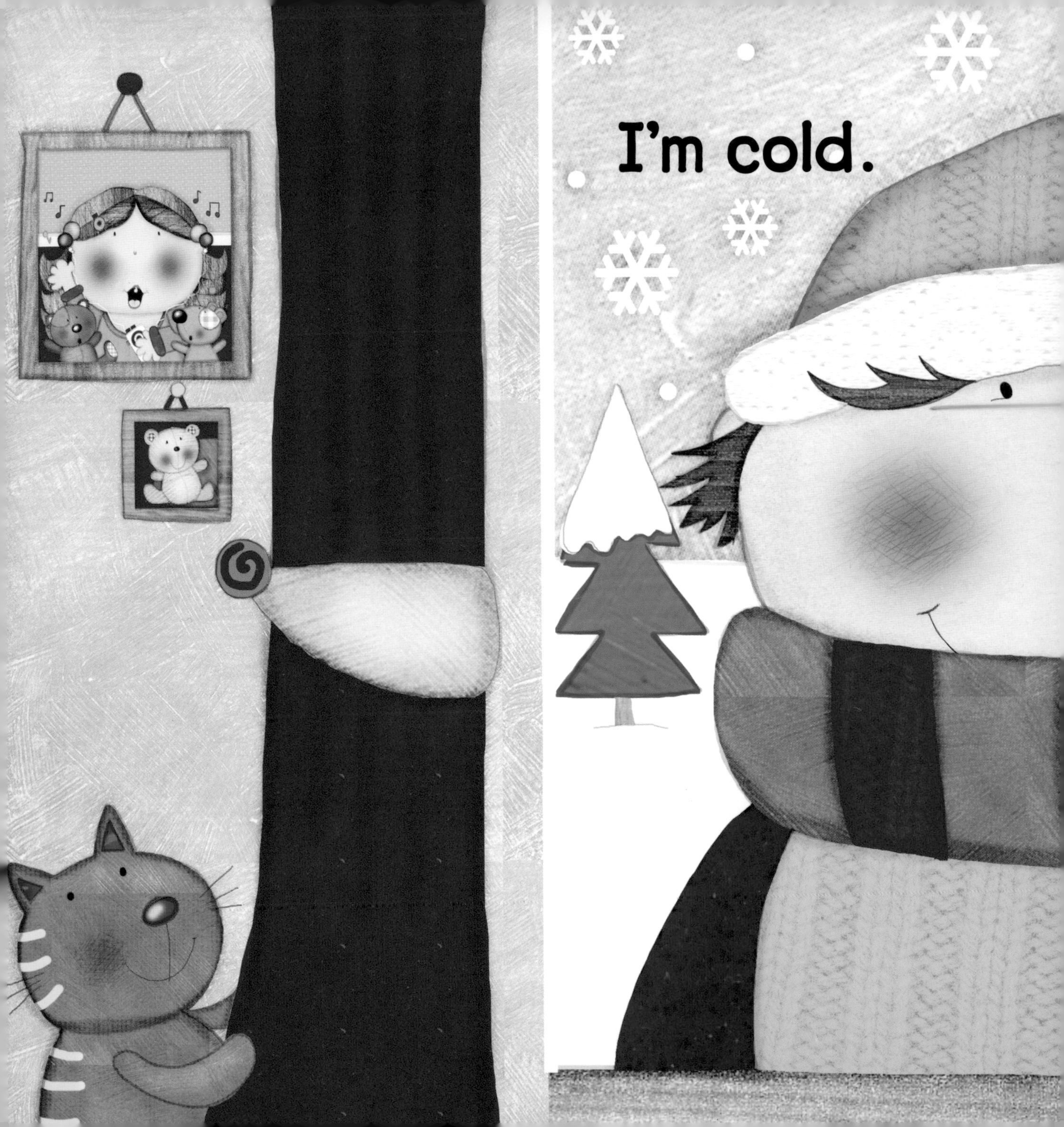

I’m cold.

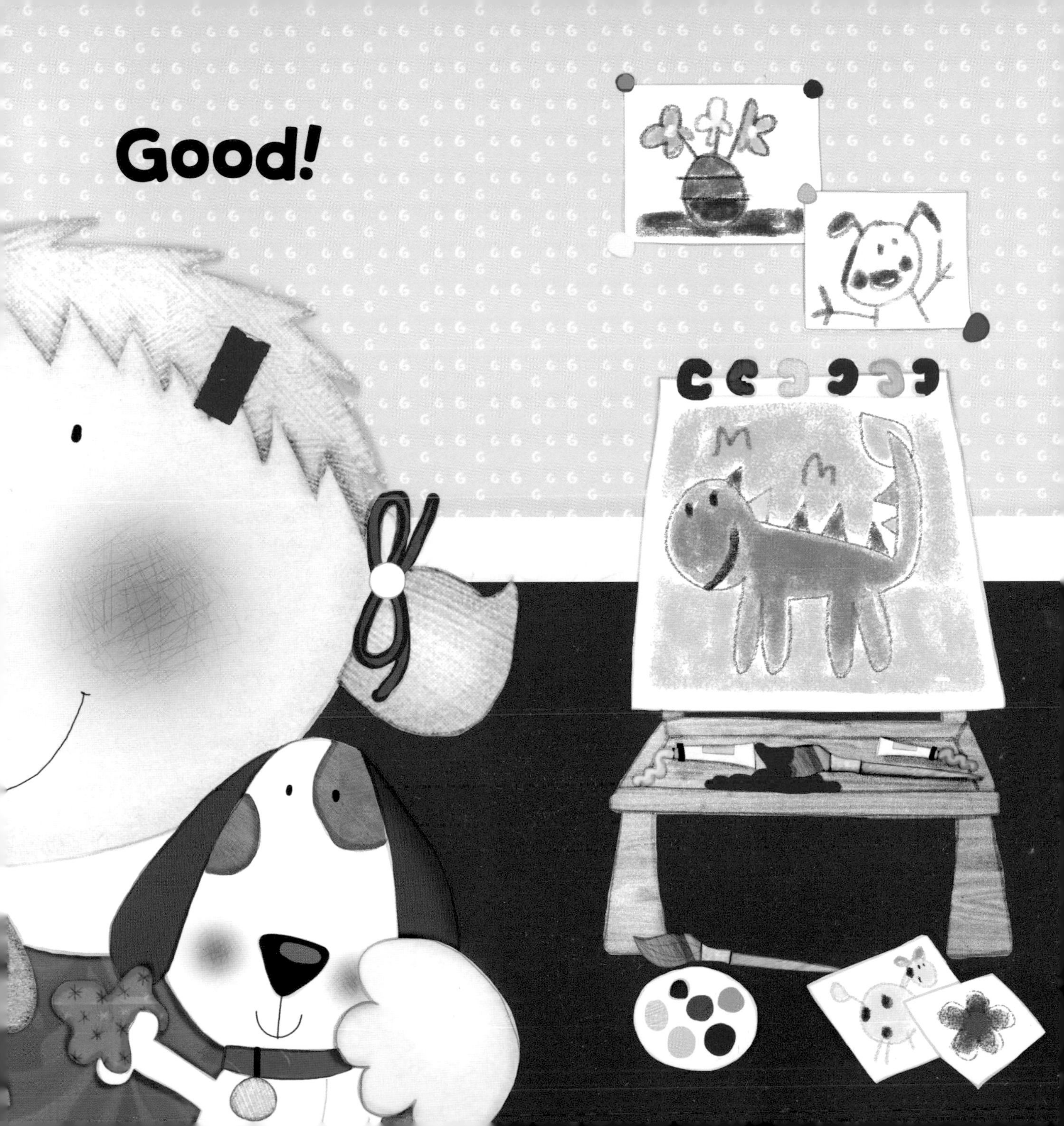
Good!

I can be noisy.

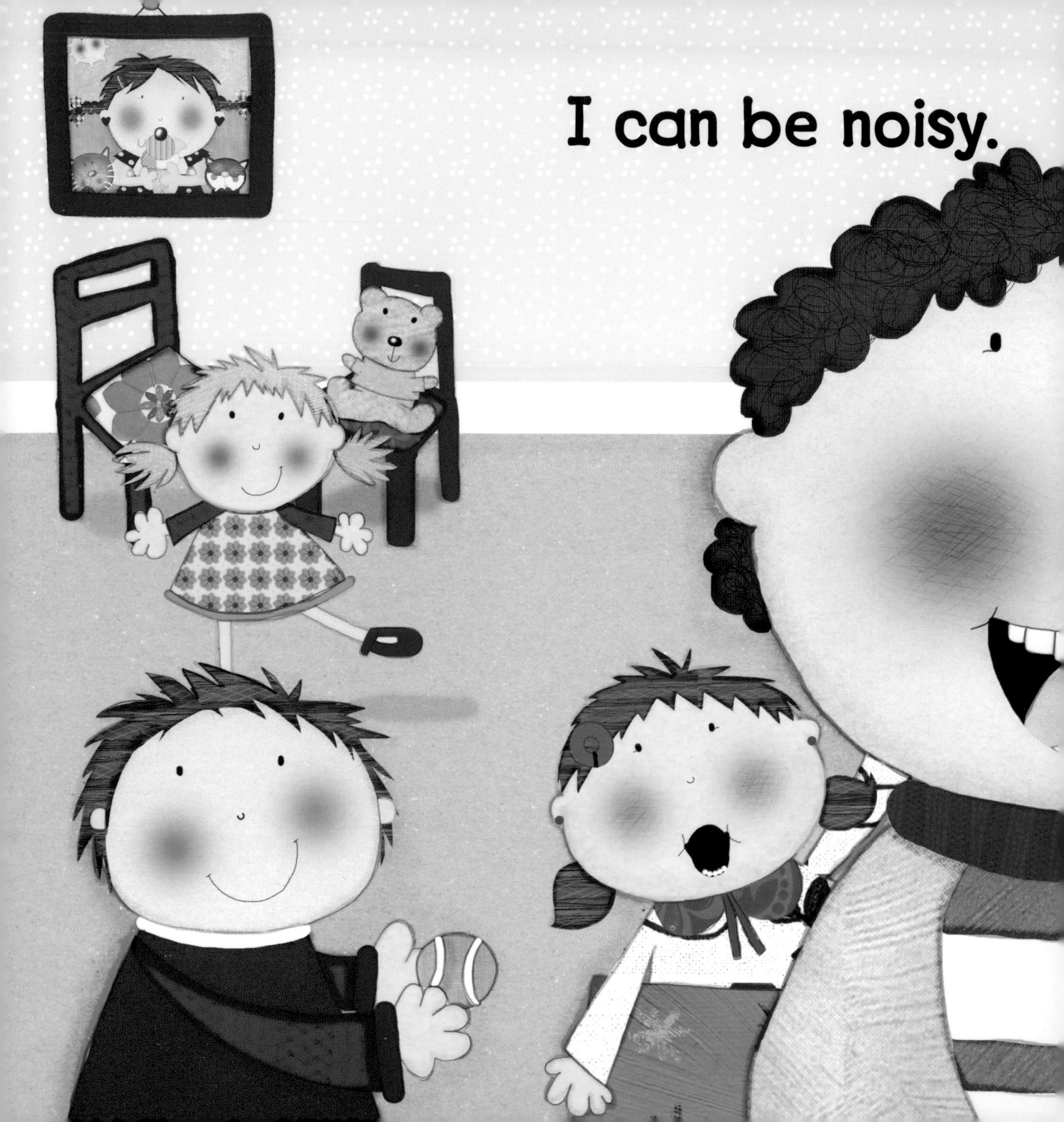

Sssh!

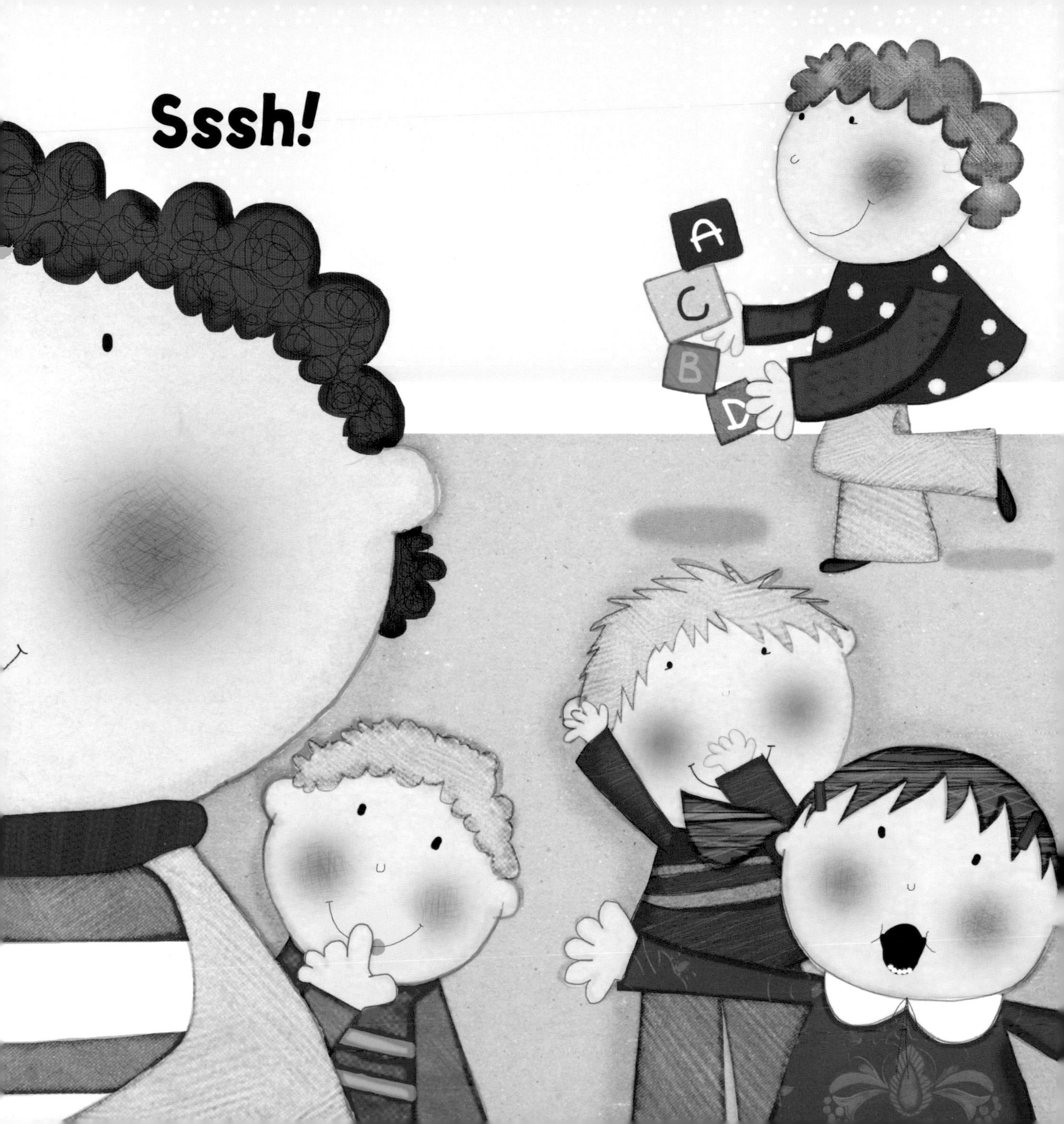

Open up. . .

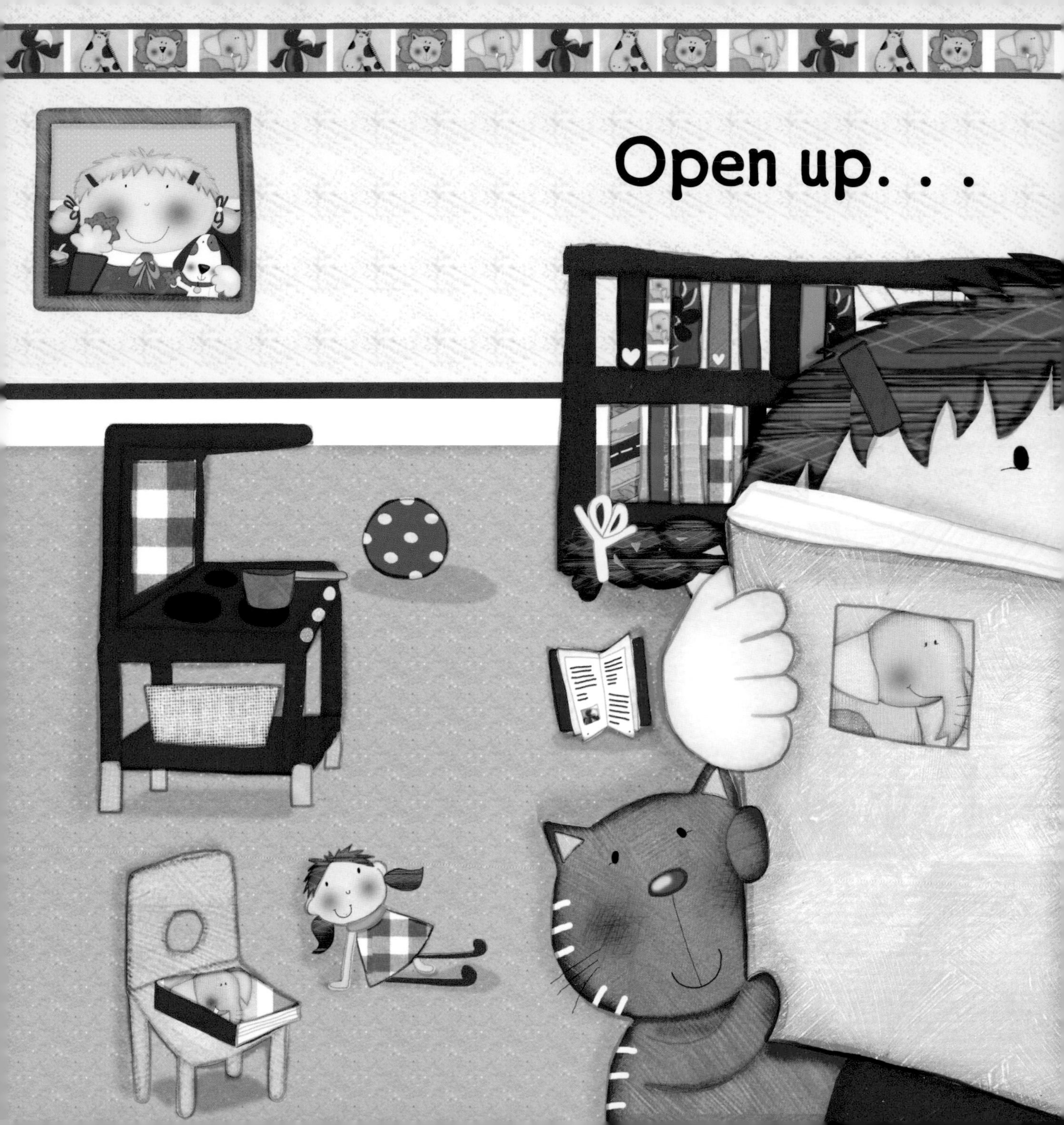